WeightWatchers®

one pot meals

Lesley Waters

SIMON & SCHUSTER
A VIACOM COMPANY

First published in Great Britain by Simon & Schuster, 1999
A Viacom Company

This edition produced for
The Book People Ltd
Hall Wood Avenue
Haydock
St Helens
WA11 9UL

First published 1997
Reprinted 2002

Simon & Schuster UK Ltd
Africa House
64–78 Kingsway
London WC2B 6AH

Design: Moore Lowenhoff
Front cover design: Zoocity
Typesetting: Stylize Digital Artwork
Photography: Steve Baxter
Styling: Marian Price
Food preparation: Jane Stevenson

ISBN 0 68485 156 3

Printed in Hong Kong

Recipe notes:
Egg size is medium, unless otherwise stated.
Vegetables are medium-sized, unless otherwise stated.
It is very important to use proper measuring spoons, not cutlery, for spoon measures.
1 tablespoon = 15 ml; 1 teaspoon = 5 ml
Dried herbs can be substituted for fresh ones, but the flavour may not always
be as good. Halve the fresh-herb quantity stated in the recipe.

Vegetarian recipes:
Ⓥ shows the recipe is vegetarian.

Contents

Introduction

Cooking great-tasting food does not require masses of pots, pans and kitchen gadgets or hours of your time! Equally, a fit and trim shape does not mean you can't enjoy your food. It's just a matter of getting the balance right.

One Pot Meals is a modern approach to cooking great family meals with a minimum of fuss. They range from super soups which may be baked in the oven to sizzling salads, which can be whipped up in a wok in no time at all. Oven-roasting, steam-frying and grilling are all covered.

There are so many advantages to cooking one pot meals – they are straightforward and simple to cook. Shopping and preparation are also a breeze and the end result leaves you with a delicious meal without a mountain of washing up!

If you get the balance right and follow the *1,2,3 Success 2000*™ Programme, you can enjoy your food and will be amazed by the family feasts which you can conjure up in one pot!

Special Cooking Method

Steam-frying

This method of cooking crops up frequently in *One Pot Cooking* and uses a non-stick pan to start to fry an ingredient, over a medium heat, until slightly coloured. Then a tablespoon of water is added, the heat is reduced slightly and the pan is covered immediately with a lid which creates steam in the pan and helps the cooking. This enables you to cook with a minimum amount of oil and maximise the flavours in your food.

Pots and Pans

One pot cooking requires only a few items of practical equipment:

- A frying-pan or large hob and oven-style shallow dish that is equally at home in the oven or on the hob.
- A non-stick wok with a lid for steam-frying, and for stews and soups.
- A chopping board and a sharp kitchen knife.

Super Soups

This chapter is not just for first courses – far from it! These soups are substantial, tasty meals in their own right. They are hearty with loads of flavour and texture, and they range from thick and creamy to spicy and chunky. Nothing is more warming or comforting than a hot bowl of soup and these recipes will satisfy you again and again.

Tomato and Basil Stew

An oven-baked chunky soup with crunchy garlic toasts.

Serves: 2
Preparation and cooking time: 35 minutes
Freezing: not recommended
Points per serving: 4
Total Points per recipe: 8
Calories per serving: 405

Ⓥ

2 teaspoons olive oil
1 onion, chopped
a pinch of sugar
1 bay leaf
1 beef tomato, chopped roughly
400 g (14 oz) canned chopped tomatoes in tomato sauce
1 small french stick, cut into 4 × 5 cm (2-inch) thick slices
1 garlic clove, peeled
2 tablespoons fresh basil leaves, torn roughly
salt and freshly ground black pepper

❶ Preheat the oven to Gas Mark 6/200°C/400°F.

❷ Heat the oil in a shallow hob and ovenproof dish. Add the onion, cover and steam-fry (see page 4) for 10 minutes or until softened. Stir in the sugar and bay leaf. Add the beef tomato and chopped tomatoes. Season well and bring to a simmer. Transfer to the oven for 10 minutes.

❸ Meanwhile lay the bread slices on a baking tray and toast in the oven for 6–7 minutes or until golden. Remove and lightly rub the warm toast with the garlic clove.

❹ Serve in a bowl and place the toasts in the soup at a vertical angle (two per person). Scatter over the basil and serve at once.

Chicken Goulash Soup with Potato Dumplings

Chicken with red pepper and aubergine topped with puffed cheesy dumplings makes a hearty and filling goulash.

Serves: 4

Preparation time: 30 minutes + 20 minutes cooking

Freezing: not recommended

Points per serving: 5¹/₂

Total Points per recipe: 22¹/₂

Calories per serving: 440

2 teaspoons olive oil or sunflower oil
1 onion, chopped
1 small aubergine, diced
1 red pepper, de-seeded and sliced thickly
4 boneless, skinless chicken thighs
1 teaspoon flour
1 tablespoon paprika
2 teaspoons coriander seeds, crushed
400 g (14 oz) canned chopped tomatoes in a rich
tomato sauce
grated rind of 1 lemon
salt and freshly ground black pepper
For the dumplings:
60 g (2¹/₄ oz) dried potato flakes
300 ml (¹/₂ pint) semi-skimmed milk or water
1 small egg, beaten
25 g (1 oz) self-raising flour
25 g (1 oz) mature Cheddar, grated
1 tablespoon parsley, chopped roughly

1 Heat the oil in a large non-stick frying-pan or wok. Add the onion, aubergine and red pepper. Cover and steam-fry over a medium heat for 6–8 minutes until well coloured.

2 Cover the thighs with non-pvc film and using a mallet or rolling pin, flatten out each chicken thigh until approximately 5 mm (¹/₄-inch) thick. Remove the film and cut each thigh in half. Remove the lid and add the chicken to the pan. Stir-fry for 1 minute.

3 Stir in the flour, paprika and coriander seeds. Fry for a further 30 seconds.

4 Add the tomatoes and lemon rind and season well. Bring to the boil, cover, and cook over a medium heat for 20 minutes.

5 For the dumplings, make the potato flakes into a mash by following the directions on the packet. Use either semi-skimmed milk or water. Cool slightly and beat in the egg, self-raising flour and cheese. Season.

6 Roll the mixture into 8 small dumplings and place on top of the soup. Spoon a little of the hot sauce from the soup over each dumpling and sprinkle with parsley. Cover again and cook for a further ten minutes over a medium heat until the dumplings are puffed and the chicken is cooked.

Weight Watchers note: if water is used instead of milk in step 5, deduct 1 Point from the total Points.

Mexican Sweetcorn and Turkey Chilli Soup

This Mexican-style chilli is fabulous with a crunchy, fresh sweetcorn and coriander salsa.

Serves: 4
Preparation time: 15 minutes + 25 minutes cooking
Freezing: not recommended
Points per serving: 7
Total Points per recipe: 28
Calories per serving: 355

1 tablespoon olive or sunflower oil
1 large onion, chopped
500 g (1 lb 2 oz) lean minced turkey
2 teaspoons ground cumin
1 teaspoon ground coriander
500 ml (18 fl oz) tomato passata
425 g (15 oz) canned kidney beans, drained
    and rinsed
1 or 2 red chillies, chopped finely or 1–2 teaspoons
    chilli sauce
300 ml (1/2 pint) turkey or chicken stock
salt and freshly ground black pepper
For the salsa:
4 spring onions with green tops, sliced
1 small red pepper, diced
175 g (6 oz) canned sweetcorn kernels, drained
3 tablespoons fresh coriander leaves, chopped
    roughly

❶ In a large non-stick frying-pan or wok, heat the oil. Add the onion and fry for 5 minutes until softened.

❷ Add the turkey mince and fry for a further 3–4 minutes. Sprinkle over the cumin and coriander and fry for 30 seconds.

❸ Stir in the passata, kidney beans and chilli and half the stock. Bring to the boil and season well.

Simmer the chilli for 20–25 minutes adding more stock gradually if the pan becomes too dry.

❹ Meanwhile, combine all the salsa ingredients together in a bowl and set to one side.

❺ To serve, ladle the chilli into 4 serving bowls and top each with a large spoonful of salsa. Serve at once.

Thick Pea Borsch

An unusual mint and carrot raita is stirred into this thick pea soup for a dynamite soup and salad combination!
Serve with hot, crunchy granary toast, remembering to add the extra Points.

Serves: 4
Preparation time: 10 minutes + 15 minutes cooking
Freezing: not recommended
Points per serving: $2^1/_2$
Total Points per recipe: 10
Calories per serving: 150

2 teaspoons olive oil or sunflower oil
1 onion, chopped roughly
500 g (1 lb 2 oz) frozen petit pois
a pinch of sugar
850 ml (1$^1/_2$ pints) vegetable stock
salt and freshly ground black pepper
For the raita:
150 ml ($^1/_4$ pint) low-fat plain yogurt

1 large carrot, peeled and grated
3 tablespoons mint leaves, chopped

❶ Heat the oil in a large non-stick frying-pan or wok. Add the onion, cover and steam-fry for 5 minutes until softened.

❷ Stir in the peas, sugar and vegetable stock. Season well and bring to the boil. Cover and simmer for 10–12 minutes.

❸ Meanwhile, in a bowl, combine all the raita ingredients together and season. Set to one side.

❹ Using a hand-held blender or liquidiser, whizz the soup until smooth. Ladle immediately into 4 serving bowls and swirl a spoonful of raita into each. Serve at once.

Mushroom, Bacon and Potato Chowder

This creamy bacon and mushroom chowder is delicious topped with fresh spinach and a squeeze of lemon juice.

Serves: 4
Preparation time: 15 minutes + 20 minutes cooking
Freezing: not recommended
Points per serving: $4^1/_2$
Total Points per recipe: $18^1/_2$
Calories per serving: 240

2 teaspoons olive oil or sunflower oil
3 rashers of lean smoked bacon, diced
1 large leek, sliced
450 g (1 lb) potatoes, scrubbed and diced coarsely

225 g (8 oz) small button mushrooms, trimmed
150 ml ($^1/_4$ pint) white wine
300 ml ($^1/_2$ pint) semi-skimmed milk
300 ml ($^1/_2$ pint) chicken stock
2 level tablespoons cornflour, mixed with a
    little water
115 g (4 oz) spinach leaves, shredded
juice of $^1/_2$ lemon
a pinch of dried nutmeg
freshly ground black pepper

❶ Heat the oil in a large non-stick frying-pan or wok. Add the bacon and leek and fry for 5 minutes.

❷ Add the potatoes and mushrooms and fry for a further minute.

❸ Stir in the wine, milk and stock and season with black pepper and a grating of nutmeg. Bring to the boil and stir in the cornflour mix. Reduce the heat and simmer for 15–20 minutes or until the potatoes are just cooked.

❹ Stir in the shredded spinach and simmer for 1 minute. Squeeze over the lemon juice and serve at once.

Thick Pea Borsch
Mushroom, Bacon and Potato Chowder

Stir It Up

The non-stick wok is a really useful piece of cooking equipment and well worth the investment. It's a great vessel for stirring up a myriad of fast, nourishing feasts in minutes and, of course, all in one pot. Remember, stir-fries don't always have to be oriental-style food; French and British-style dishes can also be swirled into life as you'll see in this chapter.

Cauliflower and Almond Madras

Cauliflower, chick-peas and coconut are the perfect combination in this vegetable curry. Serve with warm pitta breads for dunking and don't forget to count the extra Points.

Serves: 4
Preparation time: 15 minutes + 20 minutes cooking
Freezing: not recommended
Points per serving: 4¹/₂
Total Points per recipe: 17¹/₂
Calories per serving: 240

Ⓥ

2 teaspoons olive oil or sunflower oil
1 large onion, sliced
2 tablespoons Madras curry powder
1 teaspoon flour
2 tablespoons unsweetened desiccated coconut
600 ml (1 pint) hot vegetable stock
175 g (6 oz) potato, scrubbed and sliced thinly
350 g (12 oz) cauliflower florets
425 g (15 oz) canned chick-peas, drained and rinsed
15 g (¹/₂ oz) toasted flaked almonds
3 tablespoons parsley, chopped roughly
salt and freshly ground black pepper

❶ In a large non-stick frying-pan or wok, heat the oil. Fry the onion for 2–3 minutes until lightly browned. Add 1 tablespoon water, cover and steam-fry for 5 minutes until softened.

❷ Add the curry powder and flour and fry for 1 minute.

❸ Mix the desiccated coconut with the hot stock and stir into the pan. Simmer for 1 minute.

❹ Add the potato slices, cauliflower florets and chick-peas and season well. Stir together, cover and simmer for 20–25 minutes. Scatter over the almonds and parsley and serve.

Cauliflower and Almond Madras

Thai Prawns with Sugar-snap Peas

Serves: 4
Preparation time: 15 minutes + 20 minutes cooking
Freezing: not recommended
Points per serving: 4 1/2
Total Points per recipe: 17 1/2
Calories per serving: 325

2 teaspoons olive oil or sunflower oil
1 onion, chopped
1 tablespoon red Thai paste
225 g (8 oz) long-grain rice
600 ml (1 pint) vegetable stock
175 g (6 oz) sugar-snap peas, halved lengthways
100 ml (3 1/2 fl oz) vegetable stock (optional)
200 g (7 oz) frozen cooked prawns, thawed

❶ Heat the oil in a large non-stick frying-pan or wok. Add the onion, cover and steam-fry (see page 4) for 5 minutes until softened.
❷ Add the Thai paste and rice and fry, stirring, for 1 minute. Pour in 600 ml (1 pint) stock, cover and simmer for 10 minutes.
❸ Remove the lid and add the sugar-snap peas. Cover and simmer for a further 8–10 minutes until the rice and peas are cooked, adding up to 100 ml (3 1/2 fl oz) stock if the pan becomes dry.
❹ Stir through the cooked prawns and heat for 1 minute. Serve at once.

Variation: if you wish, frozen peas can be used instead of sugar-snap peas. The Points per serving will be 5 and the total Points per recipe will be 19 1/2.

Chinese Cod with Black Bean Sauce

Serves: 2
Preparation time: 15 minutes + 15 minutes cooking
Freezing: not recommended
Points per serving: 6 1/2
Total Points per recipe: 13 1/2
Calories per serving: 420

115 g (4 oz) thread egg noodles
1 teaspoon olive oil

2 × 115 g (4 oz) skinless, boneless chunky cod fillets
4 lettuce leaves (large outer leaves of a round lettuce)
1 orange, peeled and segmented
juice of 1 orange
5 tablespoons black bean sauce
freshly ground black pepper

❶ Preheat the oven to Gas Mark 6/200°C/400°F. Soak the egg noodles in boiling water, following the instructions on the packet.
❷ Meanwhile, lightly brush 2 large pieces of double-thickness tin foil (approximately 20 cm/8 inches square) with the oil and set to one side.
❸ Season each cod fillet with pepper and wrap 2 lettuce leaves around each fillet. Divide the noodles in half and place a mound in the centre of each piece of tin foil. Top each mound with a wrapped cod fillet.
❹ In a small bowl, combine the orange segments, orange juice and black bean sauce. Spoon this mixture equally over the fish.
❺ Loosely wrap the foil parcels and place on a baking tray in the oven. Bake for 10–15 minutes until the fish is cooked.
❻ To serve, place each parcel on a large dinner plate and take straight to the table.

Thai Prawns with Sugar-snap Peas
Chinese Cod with Black Bean Sauce

Broccoli, Chicken and Cashew Nut Stir-fry

The delicious combination of chicken and cashew nuts tastes even better with a twist of orange!

Serves: 4

Preparation and cooking time: 20 minutes

Freezing: not recommended

Points per serving: 7^1/$_2$

Total Points per recipe: 29^1/$_2$

Calories per serving: 425

175 g (6 oz) dried thin egg noodles
2 teaspoons olive oil or sunflower oil
1 bunch of spring onions, sliced lengthways
4 medium skinless, boneless chicken thighs,
   cut into strips
1 orange pepper, de-seeded and sliced
175 g (6 oz) broccoli florets
150 ml (^{1}/$_4$ pint) orange juice
2 teaspoons cornflour mixed with 1 tablespoon
   water
2 tablespoons soy sauce
55 g (2 oz) cashew nuts
salt and freshly ground black pepper

1 Soak the noodles in boiling water, following the directions on the packet. Meanwhile, in a large non-stick frying-pan or wok, heat the oil. Add the spring onions, cover and steam-fry (see page 4) for 2 minutes until softened.

2 Add the chicken and orange pepper, cover and steam-fry for a further 5–6 minutes, over a medium heat, stirring occasionally. The chicken should be just cooked and lightly coloured.

3 Add the broccoli, cover again and cook for 4–5 minutes. Stir in the orange juice, cornflour mix and soy sauce and season. Simmer for 1 minute. Stir in the cashew nuts and serve at once with the egg noodles.

Mustard Turkey with Green Beans

A chicken or turkey breast is complemented so well by this hot honey and mustard salad.
Delicious served with fresh crusty bread.

Serves: 4

Preparation and cooking time: 20 minutes

Freezing: not recommended

Points per serving: 3½

Total Points per recipe: 14

Calories per serving: 185

2 teaspoons olive oil or sunflower oil

350 g (12 oz) skinless, boneless turkey breast, cut into strips

juice of 1 lemon

3 tablespoons grainy mustard

2 tablespoons runny honey

115 g (4 oz) green beans, cut into 2 cm (³/₄-inch) pieces

1 tablespoon sesame seeds

salt and freshly ground black pepper

salad leaves, to serve

❶ In a large non-stick frying-pan or wok, heat the oil until very hot.

❷ In a bowl, toss together the turkey, lemon juice, mustard and honey. Season well.

❸ Add to the hot pan and stir-fry over a high heat for 3–4 minutes until the turkey is browned and nearly cooked.

❹ Stir in the beans and cook for a further 2–3 minutes. Sprinkle over the sesame seeds.

❺ Arrange the salad leaves on 4 individual serving dishes, spoon over the turkey and serve at once.

Spuds with Bacon and Spring Greens

This country-style dish with herby pan-fried new potatoes makes a complete meal.
Use new potatoes, scrub well and leave the skins on!

Serves: 3

Preparation time: 15 minutes + 25 minutes cooking

Freezing: not recommended

Points per serving: 4

Total Points per recipe: 11$^{1}/_{2}$

Calories per serving: 230

2 teaspoons olive or sunflower oil

1 red onion, cut into chunky strips

3 slices lean smoked bacon, diced

450 g (1 lb) new potatoes, halved lengthways

2 celery sticks, diced

300 ml ($^{1}/_{2}$ pint) vegetable stock

1 bay leaf

$^{1}/_{2}$ teaspoon dried mixed herbs

115 g (4 oz) spring greens, shredded

salt and freshly ground black pepper

1 Heat the oil in a large non-stick frying-pan or wok. Add the onion, cover and steam-fry (see page 4) for 5 minutes. Add the bacon, potatoes and celery, cover again and steam-fry for 2 minutes.

2 Stir in the stock, bay leaf and mixed herbs. Season. Cover and cook over a medium heat for 15–20 minutes until the potatoes are nearly cooked.

3 Stir in the spring greens and toss together with the other ingredients. Cover again and cook for a further 5 minutes. Serve at once.

Nice Rice and Perfect Pasta

Pasta and rice make excellent store cupboard ingredients. These versatile staples are a great source of energy and can, at the drop of a hat, be rustled up into a filling and wholesome meal. As a rule, choose egg-free, dried pasta, since it contains less fat and always make a point of briefly rinsing your rice before cooking since this will remove any dust and improve the texture.

Fish Lasagne

Weight Watchers tasty soups make fantastic sauces. Here you can choose either Tomato or Mushroom soup to make quick fish lasagne!

Serves: 4

Preparation time: 5 minutes + 50 minutes cooking

Freezing: not recommended

Points per serving: 4

Total Points per recipe: with tomato soup 15$^1/_2$; with mushroom soup 16

Calories per serving: 330

450 g (1 lb) frozen leaf spinach, thawed
450 g (1 lb) smoked haddock fillet, cut into chunks
2 × 295 g cans of Weight Watchers from Heinz Tomato or Mushroom soup
6 sheets, approximately 140 g (5 oz), no pre-cook lasagne
25 g (1 oz) breadcrumbs
25 g (1 oz) parmesan cheese, grated
freshly ground black pepper

1 Preheat the oven to Gas Mark 6/200°C/400°F.

2 Place half the spinach in the base of a large, shallow ovenproof dish. Top this with half the fish and then a quarter of the soup. Lay 3 sheets of lasagne on top. Season in between each layer with black pepper.

3 Next, layer on the remaining spinach, followed by the remaining fish and another quarter of the soup. Season and top with 3 more sheets of lasagne.

4 Pour over the remaining soup and lightly push down the lasagne sheets to ensure that all the lasagne is covered with soup. Sprinkle with the breadcrumbs and cheese.

5 Cover the lasagne with tin foil and bake for 35 minutes. Then remove the foil and cook for a further 10–15 minutes until browned and bubbling hot.

Roasted Vegetable Ragoût with Tagliatelle

Roasting root vegetables really intensifies their flavour and transforms the taste! Serve this ragoût topped with one of the many fresh, ready-made tomato salsas or pestos now available to buy.

Serves: 2

Preparation and cooking time: 40 minutes

Freezing: not recommended

Points per serving: if using salsa $5^1/2$; if using pesto $6^1/2$

Total Points per recipe: if using salsa 11; if using pesto 13

Calories per serving: if using salsa 515; if using pesto 530

Ⓥ

1 tablespoon olive oil
3 parsnips, diced
1 fennel bulb, diced
4 celery sticks, diced
1 onion, chopped roughly
3 large carrots, diced
600 ml (1 pint) herb stock
150 ml ($^1/_4$ pint) white wine
115 g (4 oz) quick-cook tagliatelle, broken up roughly
8 teaspoons ready-made tomato salsa or pesto, to serve
Salt and freshly ground black pepper

❶ Preheat the oven to Gas Mark 6/200°C/400°F.

❷ Heat the oil in a hob and ovenproof pan. Add the parsnips, fennel, celery, onion and carrots. Fry for 2 minutes.

❸ Transfer the pan to the oven and bake, uncovered, for 20–25 minutes.

❹ Remove the pan from the oven and place back on the hob. Pour in the stock and wine, season and bring to the boil. Simmer for 2 minutes, then stir in the tagliatelle.

❺ Cover the pan and cook for a further 4–5 minutes or until the pasta is cooked. Serve the ragoût in individual bowls topped with 2 teaspoons each of fresh tomato salsa or fresh pesto.

Bubble and Squeak Pasta

This fantastic combination of smoked bacon and sun-dried tomatoes is sure to become a favourite!

Serves: 4
Preparation and cooking time: 30 minutes
Freezing: not recommended
Points per serving: 6
Total Points per recipe: 24
Calories per serving: 455

2 teaspoons olive oil
1 onion, chopped
3 rashers lean, smoked back bacon
1 garlic clove, peeled
2 teaspoons dried thyme
350 g (12 oz) dried rigatoni pasta
4 large sun-dried tomatoes, chopped
150 ml (¼ pint) white wine
600 ml (1 pint) vegetable stock
100 ml (3½ fl oz) vegetable stock (optional)
115 g (4 oz) savoy cabbage, shredded
20 g (¾ oz) parmesan cheese, grated
salt and freshly ground black pepper

❶ Heat the oil in a large non-stick frying-pan or wok. Add the onion and bacon. Fry for 5–6 minutes until the onion is softened and the bacon is lightly coloured.

❷ Add the garlic and thyme and fry for 1 minute. Stir in the pasta, sun-dried tomatoes, wine and 600 ml (1 pint) vegetable stock. Season well and cover. Cook over a medium heat for 12 minutes or until the pasta is cooked. Add a little more stock if the pan becomes too dry.

❸ 5 minutes before the end of the cooking time, stir in the shredded cabbage.

❹ To serve, sprinkle with the parmesan cheese, toss together and serve at once.

Variation: if you don't have rigatoni, any other dried pasta shapes or shells would work well too.

Bubble and Squeak Pasta

Orange Lentils with Mediterranean Lamb

Garlic and rosemary are the classic accompaniments for lamb. Add some orange lentils and brown rice and you have a hearty supper!

Serves: 4
Preparation time: 20 minutes + 40 minutes cooking
Freezing: not recommended
Points per serving: 7¹/₂
Total Points per recipe: 31
Calories per serving: 505

2 teaspoons olive oil
280 g (10 oz) leeks, sliced and washed

350 g (12 oz) lean lamb leg steak, cubed
2 garlic cloves, crushed
2 teaspoons dried rosemary
225 g (8 oz) easy-cook brown rice
115 g (4 oz) orange lentils, rinsed
1 yellow pepper, cut into strips (optional)
600 ml (1 pint) vegetable stock
300 ml (¹/₂ pint) vegetable stock (optional)
salt and freshly ground black pepper

❶ Heat the oil in large non-stick pan. Add the leeks, cover and steam-fry (see page 4) for 10 minutes until softened.
❷ Remove the lid, add the lamb, garlic and rosemary and fry for 2–3 minutes. Stir in the rice, lentils, yellow pepper and 600 ml (1 pint) of the stock. Season well and bring to the boil.
❸ Cover and simmer for 30–40 minutes until the rice is cooked. Stir occasionally and add more stock if the pan becomes too dry.

Kedgeree

Canned long-grain rice really speeds up this recipe for classic kedgeree.

Serves: 4
Preparation and cooking time: 15 minutes
Freezing: not recommended
Points per serving: with egg 6; without egg 5¹/₂
Total Points per recipe: with egg 24¹/₂; without egg 21¹/₂
Calories per serving: with egg 345; without egg 300

2 teaspoons olive oil or sunflower oil
1 onion, sliced

2 tablespoons mild curry paste
275 g (9¹/₂ oz) canned long-grain rice
300 ml (¹/₂ pint) vegetable stock
425 g (15 oz) canned red salmon, drained with the juice reserved
juice and grated rind of 1 lemon
3 tablespoons chopped fresh parsley
2 hard-boiled eggs, peeled and chopped (optional)
salt and freshly ground black pepper

❶ Heat the oil in a large non-stick frying-pan or wok. Add the onion and steam-fry (see page 4) for 5 minutes until softened. Add in the curry paste and cook for 30 seconds.
❷ Stir in the rice, stock and reserved salmon juice. Season. Cover and simmer for 3 minutes. Stir in the salmon and lemon juice. Heat through.
❸ Scatter over the lemon rind, parsley and chopped egg, if using, and serve at once.

Variation: tuna can be used instead of red salmon. The Points per serving will be 5 and the total Points per recipe will be 19¹/₂.

Orange Lentils with Mediterranean Lamb
Kedgeree

Baked Fruit Pilaff with Chicken

Baking whole lemon pieces really gets the most out of a lemon's flavour and juice. In this dish,
it makes a delicious sauce for the chicken and rice.

Serves: 2
Preparation time: 20 minutes + 35 minutes cooking
Freezing: not recommended
Points per serving: 8¹/₂
Total Points per recipe: 17¹/₂
Calories per serving: 575

2 teaspoons olive oil or sunflower oil
1 onion, chopped
¹/₂ teaspoon cumin
¹/₂ teaspoon ground coriander
¹/₂ teaspoon cinnamon
1 teaspoon turmeric
1 garlic clove, crushed
175 g (6 oz) long-grain rice
25 g (1 oz) sultanas
55 g (2 oz) dried, ready-to-eat prunes, chopped
    roughly
450 ml (16 fl oz) vegetable stock
¹/₂ lemon, cut in half
2 small chicken breasts
1 teaspoon honey
salt and freshly ground black pepper

1 Preheat the oven to Gas Mark 6/200°C/400°F.
2 Heat the oil in a hob and oven-proof dish. Add the onion and fry for 5 minutes. Add the spices and fry for a further 30 seconds. Stir in the garlic, rice, sultanas, prunes and vegetable stock. Squeeze over the juice from the lemon pieces, then add the lemon pieces to the pan.
3 Season well and bring the contents of the pan to the boil. Simmer for 1 minute, then cover and transfer to the oven for 15 minutes.
4 Cover the chicken with non-pvc film and using a mallet or rolling pin, flatten out the chicken breasts until they are approximately 1 cm (¹/₂-inch) thick.

Using a sharp knife, cut each breast in half and score each piece in a criss-cross pattern, taking care not to cut all the way through the chicken breast. Season and set to one side.
5 Drizzle the scored chicken pieces with the honey. Remove the dish from the oven and place the chicken pieces on the rice, pushing them down slightly into the surface of the rice. Use 2 teaspoons to carefully pick up the cooked lemon pieces in the pan and squeeze out any remaining lemon juice over the chicken and rice.
6 Return the dish to the oven for 15–20 minutes until the chicken is cooked.

Sizzling Salads

Gone are the days of the cold and dull salad plate, full of limp lettuce and acid beetroot. Salads are delicious, substantial meals in the main and can be served all the year round with a wide variety of exciting and interesting ingredients. In this chapter, vegetables, fish, meat and grains are used to create tasty dishes which can be served cold or sizzling hot, tossed in a flavoursome dressing.

Caesar and Roasted Potato Salad

Weight Watchers mayonnaise-style dressing keeps the Points low but really enhances the delicious flavours of roasted new potatoes and bacon.

Serves: 2
Preparation and cooking time: 25 minutes
Freezing: not recommended
Points per serving: 6
Total Points per recipe: 12
Calories per serving: 270

550 g (1 lb 4 oz) canned, unpeeled new potatoes, drained and rinsed (and halved if large)
1/2 red onion, sliced
1 rasher of lean, smoked back bacon, cut into thin strips
1 tablespoon olive oil
3 tablespoons Weight Watchers from Heinz mayonnaise-style dressing
juice of 1 lemon
1 small garlic clove, crushed
1 small cos lettuce or romaine lettuce
2 tablespoons chives, chopped roughly
freshly ground black pepper

1 Preheat the oven to Gas Mark 6/200°C /400°F.

2 In a non-stick roasting tin, toss together the new potatoes, onion, bacon and oil. Season with black pepper. Roast in the oven for 15–20 minutes.

3 Meanwhile, combine the mayonnaise-style dressing with the juice of 1/2 the lemon. Add the garlic and season with black pepper.

4 Reserve some of the large outer leaves of the lettuce and shred the remainder.

5 Toss the dressing with the hot potato mixture. Using the large lettuce leaves as a shell, pile in some of the shredded lettuce. Top with the hot potato mixture and squeeze over a little extra lemon juice. Sprinkle with the chives and serve at once.

Baked Roasted Vegetables with Hummous Toasts

Baking gives an intensely sweet flavour to these colourful vegetables. Serve with low-fat hummous and sesame toasts for a memorable feast!

Serves: 4

Preparation time: 5 minutes + 50 minutes cooking

Freezing: not recommended

Points per serving: 3

Total Points per recipe: 11½

Calories per serving: 220

Ⓥ

2 courgettes, cut into 2.5 cm (1-inch) chunks

1 large aubergine, cut into 2.5 cm (1-inch) chunks

1 red pepper, cut into 2.5 cm (1-inch) chunks

1 yellow pepper, cut into 2.5 cm (1-inch) chunks

2 red onions, cut into wedges

1 tablespoon olive oil

2 tablespoons fresh thyme

50 ml (2 fl oz) herb vegetable stock

75 ml (2¾ oz) herb vegetable stock (optional)

2 tablespoons balsamic vinegar

4 medium slices of country-style bread

4 tablespoons low-fat hummous

2 teaspoons toasted sesame seeds

salt and freshly ground black pepper

❶ Preheat the oven to Gas Mark 6/200°C/400°F.

❷ In a non-stick roasting pan, toss all the vegetables together with the oil and thyme. Season well and pour over 50 ml (2 fl oz) of the stock. Bake the vegetables in the oven for 50–60 minutes until tender and slightly browned. Add up to 75 ml (2¾ fl oz) more stock if the roasting tin becomes too dry.

❸ Remove from the oven and stir in the balsamic vinegar.

❹ Place the bread slices in the oven to toast. Spread each toasted slice with some hummous and sprinkle with the toasted sesame seeds. Serve the warm roasted vegetables with the hummous toasts.

Baked Roasted Vegetables with Hummous Toasts
Caesar and Roasted Potato Salad (page 27)

Tomato, Mint and Lentil Salad

Canned lentils are a wonderful and quick alternative to the dried ones. Hot and Spicy Croûtes (below) are delicious with this.

Serves: 4
Preparation and cooking time: 20 minutes
Freezing: not recommended
Points per serving: 2¹/₂
Total Points per recipe: 11
Calories per serving: 130

2 teaspoons olive oil
1 large onion, diced
1 rasher of lean smoked back bacon, diced
200 ml (7 fl oz) tomato passata
425 g (15 oz) canned green lentils, drained and
   rinsed
2 tablespoons roughly chopped fresh mint
115 g (4 oz) cherry tomatoes, halved
4 thick slices of iceberg lettuce
salt and freshly ground black pepper

❶ Heat the oil in a non-stick frying-pan. Add the onion and bacon and fry gently for 10 minutes until softened and lightly coloured.

❷ Add the tomato passata to the pan and season well. Simmer for 2 minutes.

❸ Add the lentils and mint and toss together well. Carefully stir in the cherry tomatoes.

❹ Place a slice of iceberg lettuce on each serving plate and pile the salad on top to serve.

Hot and Spicy Croûtes

These are the perfect accompaniment to tomato, mint and lentil salad and many other dishes!

Serves: 4
Preparation and cooking time: 10 minutes
Freezing: not recommended
Points per serving: 1
Total Points per recipe: 5
Calories per serving: 80

8 × 1 cm (¹/₂-inch) thick slices of French stick
2 teaspoons olive oil
¹/₄ teaspoon ground cumin
¹/₄ teaspoon ground coriander
¹/₄ teaspoon paprika

Ⓥ

❶ Preheat the oven to Gas Mark 6/200°C/400°F.

❷ Brush the bread on each side with a little oil and place on a baking sheet.

❸ In a bowl, toss the spices together and sprinkle over the top side of the bread.

❹ Bake in the oven for 5–8 minutes until toasted and golden. Serve warm.

Tomato, Mint and Lentil Salad

Spiced Turkey Salad Tortillas

Serves: 4
Preparation and cooking time: 25 minutes
  + 1 hour marinating
Freezing: not recommended
Points per serving: 5¹/₂
Total Points per recipe: 22¹/₂
Calories per serving: 280

250 g (9 oz) turkey breast
1 onion, cut into wedge-like strips
1 tablespoon olive oil
juice of 1 lemon
1 teaspoon hot chilli powder
2 teaspoons ground cumin
salt and freshly ground black pepper
To serve:
4 large flour tortillas
4 handfuls of crunchy salad leaves, shredded
1 small red pepper, cut into strips
115 g (4 oz) canned baby sweetcorn, drained
    and rinsed
2 tablespoons low-fat plain yogurt
lime wedges

❶ Cover the turkey with non-pvc film and with a mallet or rolling pin, flatten the turkey until it is thin and then cut it into rough pieces. In a large bowl, toss together the turkey, onion, ¹/₂ tablespoon oil, lemon juice, chilli powder and cumin. Season and set to one side to marinate for an hour.

❷ Warm the tortillas according to the packet instructions. Meanwhile, heat the remaining ¹/₂ tablespoon oil in a non-stick frying-pan. Pour in the turkey mixture with all its marinade and fry for 2 minutes. Cover the pan with a lid and simmer for 4–5 minutes, until the turkey is cooked.

❸ To serve, allow each person to place some crisp salad leaves, red pepper and baby sweetcorn on a warm tortilla. Top each one with some spiced turkey and a blob of yogurt. Squeeze some lime juice over each and wrap up to eat. Garnish each plate with a lime wedge.

Warm Cannellini Salad with Beetroot Relish (page 34)
Spiced Turkey Salad Tortillas

Warm Cannellini Salad with Beetroot Relish

This fabulous bean and beetroot combination tastes best when piled on to warm crusty bread!

Serves: 4

Preparation and cooking time: 5 minutes
+ 1 hour marinating

Freezing: not recommended

Points per serving: 5

Total Points per recipe: 19½

Calories per serving: 280

1 tablespoon olive oil
4 celery sticks, diced (leaves reserved for garnish)
6 large spring onions with green tops, sliced
1 large garlic clove, crushed
85 ml (3 fl oz) herb stock
800 g (1 lb 12 oz) canned cannellini beans,
    drained and rinsed
200 g (7 oz) canned skinless, boneless red
    salmon, flaked roughly
2 tablespoons low-fat fromage frais
salt and freshly ground black pepper
celery leaves, to garnish
For the beetroot relish:
200 g (7 oz) cooked beetroot, diced
juice of ½ lemon
1 teaspoon sugar
1 teaspoon coriander seeds, crushed
2 tablespoons flat-leaf parsley, chopped roughly

1 To make the hot dressing, heat the oil in a non-stick pan. Add the celery and fry gently for 5 minutes. Add the spring onions and garlic and fry for a further minute. Pour in the stock and season well. Simmer for 1 minute.

2 Place the cannellini beans in a large bowl. Pour over the hot dressing and gently toss together. Set aside to marinate for an hour.

3 Combine all the ingredients for the relish together, season well and set to one side.

4 To serve, gently stir the salmon into the dressed cannellini beans. Spoon into four serving bowls and top each with some of the beetroot relish. Top with a blob of fromage frais, add the celery leaves and serve at once.

Crust and Crumb

This chapter will enable you to make fresh, savoury pies and crumbles which aren't laden with greasy pastry and unwanted Points and Calories. Ranging from a tasty Thai chicken crumble to a herby upside-down pizza, these dishes offer a wide variety of flavours and textures which the whole family can enjoy.

Smoked Mackerel and Horseradish Bread Pudding

A savoury version of a traditional pud!

Serves: 3
Preparation time: 10 minutes + 30 minutes standing + 30 minutes cooking
Freezing: not recommended
Points per serving: 9½
Total Points per recipe: 29
Calories per serving: 710

3 large slices of granary bread, quartered
225 g (8 oz) skinless, boneless peppered mackerel fillets, flaked
2 eggs
425 ml (15 fl oz) skimmed milk
3 tablespoons low-fat milk powder
2 tablespoons horseradish, to taste
To serve:
crisp salad leaves
1 lemon, cut into wedges

❶ Lay the bread quarters in a 1.7 litre (3 pint) shallow ovenproof dish. Scatter over the flaked mackerel.

❷ In a bowl, whisk together the eggs, milk, milk powder and horseradish. Pour this over the bread and mackerel and set to one side to stand for 30 minutes.

❸ Preheat the oven to Gas Mark 5/190°C/375°F.

❹ Bake for approximately 30 minutes until puffed, firm and lightly golden. Serve at once with the crisp salad leaves. Place a lemon wedge on each plate and squeeze over the dish.

Green Thai Chicken Crumble

Be careful when adding the Thai paste as some brands can be very spicy!

Serves: 4 (for lunch) or 2 (for dinner)
Preparation and cooking time: 40 minutes
Freezing: not recommended
Points per serving: 5¹/₂ for 4; 11 for 2
Total Points per recipe: 22
Calories per serving: 300

2 teaspoons sunflower oil
1 onion, chopped
4 skinless, boneless chicken thighs, diced into
    2.5 cm (1 inch) pieces
3 teaspoons green Thai paste (or to taste)
4 level teaspoons flour
300 ml (¹/₂ pint) semi-skimmed milk
300 ml (¹/₂ pint) chicken stock
225 g (8 oz) broccoli florets
115 g (4 oz) frozen peas
40 g (1¹/₂ oz) breadcrumbs (made with 1-day-old
    bread)
1 tablespoon unsweetened desiccated coconut
salt and freshly ground black pepper

❶ Preheat the oven to Gas Mark 6/200°C/400°F.

❷ Heat the oil in a large and shallow non-stick pan. Add the onion, cover and steam-fry (see page 4) for 5 minutes. Add the chicken, cover and steam-fry for a further 3 minutes. Remove the lid and add the Thai paste. Fry for 30 seconds, then stir in the flour and fry for a further 30 seconds.

❸ Remove the pan from the heat and gradually stir in the milk and chicken stock. Season well and return to the heat. Bring to the boil, stirring occasionally and simmer for 8 minutes.

❹ Add the broccoli florets to the pan, cover and simmer for 2 minutes. Then add the peas and simmer for a further 2 minutes.

❺ Meanwhile, in a bowl, combine the breadcrumbs with the desiccated coconut. Sprinkle this mix over the surface of the Thai chicken and transfer the uncovered pan to the oven for 10–12 minutes until the crumble is lightly browned.

Mixed Bean and Chilli Con Carne Pie

Taco shells provide a deliciously crunchy topping for this bean pie.

Serves: 4

Preparation time: 15 minutes + 30 minutes cooking

Freezing: not recommended

Points per serving: 8¹/₂

Total Points per recipe: 33¹/₂

Calories per serving: 370

2 teaspoons sunflower oil

1 onion, chopped

450 g (1 lb) lean minced pork

2 teaspoons cumin

1 garlic clove

425 g (15 oz) canned borlotti beans, drained and rinsed

200 g (7 oz) canned kidney beans, drained and rinsed

400 ml (14 fl oz) tomato passata

300 ml (¹/₂ pint) vegetable stock

3 taco shells, broken up coarsely

25 g (1 oz) reduced-fat Cheddar, grated

salt and freshly ground black pepper

❶ Preheat the oven to Gas Mark 5/190°C/375°F.

❷ Heat the oil in a dish which can go on the hob and in the oven. Add the onion and fry for five minutes until softened. Stir in the pork, cumin and garlic. Fry, stirring, for a further 2–3 minutes.

❸ Stir in the borlotti and kidney beans, tomato passata and stock. Season well. Bring to a simmer and remove from the heat. Scatter over the bits of taco shells and grated cheese and immediately transfer to the oven. Bake for 30 minutes until bubbling hot.

Variation: for a change, leave the taco shells whole and fill with the baked chilli.

Greek Lamb and Vegetable Flat Strudel

This flat strudel is layered rather than rolled. It is quick and simple to prepare with a light, crisp result!

Serves: 4

Preparation time: 5 minutes + 30 minutes standing
+ 40 minutes cooking

Freezing: not recommended

Points per serving: 7^1/$_2$

Total Points per recipe: 29

Calories per serving: 335

1 onion, diced
1 large courgette, diced
2 teaspoons dried oregano
2 garlic cloves, crushed
juice of 1 lemon
350 g (12 oz) lean minced lamb
5 tablespoons vegetable purée
8 sheets of filo pastry, approximately 200 g (7 oz)
2 tablespoons skimmed milk
1 egg, beaten
1 teaspoon sesame seeds
salt and freshly ground black pepper

❶ In a bowl, combine the onion, courgette, oregano, garlic and lemon juice. Set to one side for 30 minutes.

❷ Preheat the oven to Gas Mark 5/190°C/375°F.

❸ Add the lamb and the vegetable purée to the vegetable mixture above and mix together. Season well.

❹ On a non-stick baking sheet, layer up 4 sheets of the filo pastry, lightly brushing each sheet with 1 tablespoon of skimmed milk. Carefully spread the lamb and vegetable mixture evenly over the pastry. Top with the remaining 4 sheets of filo and lightly brush between each sheet with the remaining skimmed milk.

❺ Brush the top of the pie with the beaten egg, and using a sharp knife, cut through the top layer in a criss-cross fashion. Sprinkle over the sesame seeds and bake for 40–45 minutes until golden brown and cooked.

Roast Chicken with Carrot and Poppyseed Stuffing

Sunday lunch with all the trimmings!

Serves: 4

Preparation time: 15 minutes + 2 hours cooking

Freezing: not recommended

Points per serving: 4$^1/_2$

Total Points per recipe: 17$^1/_2$

Calories per serving: 495

1.3 kg (3 lb) roasting chicken

2 lemons, halved

1 bay leaf

4 large garlic cloves

12 very small potatoes approximately 50 g (1³/₄ oz)
**   each, washed well**

150 ml (¹/₄ pint) herb or vegetable stock

salt and freshly ground black pepper

For the stuffing:

115 g (4 oz) fresh breadcrumbs

1 large carrot, grated

3 teaspoons poppyseeds

1 onion, grated

grated zest and juice of 1 small orange

1 celery stick, chopped very finely

1 egg white, beaten

❶ Preheat the oven to Gas Mark 6/200°C/400°F.

❷ Using sharp kitchen scissors, remove the backbone from the chicken. Pull the chicken open slightly and lay the chicken, skin-side down, in a large roasting tin. Squeeze over the juice of 1 lemon and place the squeezed halves in the upturned cavity along with the bay leaf. Season well and roast in the oven for 40 minutes.

❸ Meanwhile, combine all the stuffing ingredients in a bowl and season well.

❹ Carefully lift the chicken out of the roasting tin after it has roasted for 40 minutes and transfer to a plate, skin-side up. Drain off any fat from the tin and, using your hands, place the stuffing in a mound, approximately the size of the chicken cavity, on the base of the tin.

❺ Take the chicken and place it skin-side up on top of the stuffing. Season again and squeeze over the juice from the remaining lemon halves. Surround the chicken with the garlic cloves, potatoes and squeezed lemon halves. Pour in the stock.

❻ Return to the oven for a further 60–90 minutes, until the potatoes are cooked and the chicken juices run clear.

Upside-down Pizza Pie

This tasty pizza is full of flavour – roasted peppers with garlic and cheese are a truly wonderful combination.

Serves: 4

Preparation time: 40 minutes + 15 minutes cooking

Freezing: not recommended

Points per serving: with low-fat soft cheese 4^1/$_2$; with low-fat fromage frais 3; with low-fat quark 3

Total Points per recipe: with low-fat soft cheese 13^1/$_2$; with low-fat fromage frais 12^1/$_2$; with low-fat quark 11^1/$_2$

Calories per serving: with low-fat soft cheese 205; with low-fat fromage frais 175; with low-fat quark 185

Ⓥ if using vegetarian cheese

1 tablespoon olive oil

2 red peppers, de-seeded and halved

1 orange pepper, de-seeded and halved

1 yellow pepper, de-seeded and halved

1 large red onion, cut into wedge-like strips

145 g packet of pizza base mix

1 large garlic clove, crushed

1 teaspoon dried mixed herbs

115 g (4 oz) low-fat soft cheese, fromage frais or quark

salt and freshly ground black pepper

❶ Preheat the oven to Gas Mark 6/200°C/400°F.

❷ Rub the oil over the base of a shallow and round baking tin, approximately 24 cm (9^1/$_2$ inches) in diameter. Lay the pepper halves on the base, skin-side down and scatter over the onion strips. Season well.

❸ Bake in the oven for 25 minutes until the peppers are slightly charred.

❹ Meanwhile, make up the pizza dough as directed on the packet, kneading in the crushed garlic. Roll out into a large, thin circle, large enough to cover the peppers.

❺ Remove the lightly charred peppers from the oven and sprinkle with the mixed herbs. Take the circle of dough and lay it over the peppers and onions. Return the pizza pie to the oven for a further 12–15 minutes until the dough is risen and golden.

❻ Remove from the oven and turn the pizza out, upside-down, on to a large serving plate or board. Place blobs of the cheese over the peppers and serve at once.

Pudding Pots

Puddings don't have to be complicated or full of fat to taste great. Just try the recipes for Chocolate Mousse and Hot Strawberry Cream Trifle and you'll see how true it is. All these scrumptious puds can be made with very little time and effort so you can whip them up on a whim if you fancy something a little indulgent.

Not-so-naughty Chocolate Mousse

Serves: 4

Points per serving: 4

Total Points per recipe: 17

Calories per serving: 240

Ⓥ

Simmer 175 g (6 oz) pre-soaked prunes in a little water until very soft. Transfer to a processor and blend until smooth. In a bowl, whisk 3 egg whites until stiff, then whisk in 3 teaspoons caster sugar until thick and glossy. Lightly fold together the puréed prunes, whisked eggs and sugar and 115 g (4 oz) melted chocolate. Transfer the chocolate mousse to 4 individual serving glasses and chill until required.

Nectarine Smoothie

Serves: 2

Points per serving: 2

Total Points per recipe: 4^1/$_2$

Calories per serving: 105

In a food processor or liquidiser, place 2 large, ripe stoned nectarines, 1 large peeled orange, 50 ml (2 fl oz) water and a squeeze of lemon juice. Whizz until smooth. Pour into 2 soup bowls, swirl a tablespoonful of low-fat plain fromage frais over each. Roughly smash a ready-made meringue nest and top each smoothie with some crumbled meringue and a spoonful of canned raspberries.

Not-so-naughty Chocolate Mousse
Nectarine Smoothie

Tropical Parcels

Serves: 4
Points per serving: 3
Ⓥ

Total Points per recipe: 12¹/₂
Calories per serving: 245

Preheat the oven to Gas Mark 6/200°C/400°F. Use 400 g (14 oz) canned drained mango slices, juice reserved, 400 g (14 oz) canned drained lychees and 1 large sliced ripe banana. Divide the fruits between 4 double thickness squares of tin foil approximately 15 cm (6 inches) square, placing them in the centre of each square. Spoon 1 tablespoon of the reserved mango juice over each and top with a fresh lime wedge. Enclose the parcels and bake in the oven for 10–15 minutes. Squeeze over the hot lime and serve with a 60 g (2¹/₄ oz) scoop of Weight Watchers from Heinz Iced Vanilla Dessert.

Hot Strawberry Cream Trifle

Serves: 2
Points per serving: 5
Ⓥ

Total Points per recipe: 10
Calories per serving: 135

Gently heat the juice of a large orange with 115 g (4 oz) quartered strawberries. Take 2 serving glasses and roughly crumble 3 sponge fingers into the base of each. Top with a generous spoonful of Weight Watchers from Heinz Iced Vanilla Dessert. Spoon over the hot strawberries with all their juice and add a sprig of mint.

Blackened Baked Banana with Cream and Maple

Serves: 1
Points per serving: 2¹/₂
Ⓥ if using gelatine-free crème fraîche

Total Points per recipe: 2¹/₂
Calories per serving: 155

Preheat the oven to Gas Mark 6/200°C/400°F. Place a large banana on a baking tray and bake in the oven for 12–15 minutes until blackened. Remove and cut down the side to split open. Spoon 2 teaspoons of low-fat crème fraîche into the split and drizzle over a teaspoon of maple syrup or a little runny honey.

Instant Iced Berries

Serves: 4
Points per serving: 1

Total Points per recipe: 3¹/₂
Calories per serving: 60

Take a 450 g (1 lb) bag of frozen berry fruit mix and thaw slightly. Place in a food processor with approximately 2 teaspoons icing sugar. Whizz briefly, add 2 tablespoons Greek-style yogurt and whizz again briefly. Serve at once!

Instant Iced Berries
Blackened Baked Banana with Cream and Maple

Index

Weight Watchers®

pizza toppings
& pasta sauces

Liz Trigg

SIMON & SCHUSTER
A VIACOM COMPANY

First published in Great Britain by Simon and Schuster, 1998
A Viacom Company

This edition produced for
The Book People Ltd
Hall Wood Avenue
Haydock
St Helens
WA11 9UL

First published 1998
Reprinted 2002

Simon & Schuster UK Ltd
Africa House
64–78 Kingsway
London WC2B 6AH

Design: Moore Lowenhoff
Cover design: Zoocity
Typesetting: Stylize
Photography: Karl Adamson
Styling: Jo Harris
Food preparation: Shirley Gill

ISBN 0-68481-953-8

Printed in Hong Kong

Recipe notes:
Egg size is medium, unless otherwise stated.
Vegetables are medium-sized, unless otherwise stated.
It is very important to use proper measuring spoons, not cutlery, for spoon measures.
1 tablespoon = 15 ml; 1 teaspoon = 5 ml
Dried herbs can be substituted for fresh ones, but the flavour may not always
be as good. Halve the fresh-herb quantity stated in the recipe.

Vegetarian recipes:
Ⓥ shows the recipe is vegetarian.

Contents

Introduction

Pizza originated in Italy, but it has become a truly international food, enjoyed by people all over the world and is without a doubt one of the most popular dishes around. Pizza is very versatile and adaptable, so it's fun to make and experiment with. It is also a convenient meal in itself; the bread base, which is usually topped with a variety of meat and vegetables and then covered in cheese, is filling and a favourite family treat. Hot melted cheese is essential, but it is also something to watch when counting Points! If you decide to create your own variations, use a half-fat mozzarella cheese, finely grated, to help keep the Points low. Also, feel free to use as many different vegetables as you wish and use the Point-free Basic Tomato Sauce (page 6) – so much better than the ready-made pizza sauces in the supermarket which can be high in Points. Those of you who have time may want to prepare a batch of tomato sauce and then freeze it in useful quantities. Always cook pizzas on a heavy baking sheet in a preheated oven and serve them as soon as they come out of the oven.

Pasta is the other famous Italian contribution to the world's cuisine. Where would we be without it? It is quick and easy to make and can be prepared in so many different, delicious ways. Dried pasta is easy to store and cook but fresh pasta is a real treat and can be an even speedier option. The recipes here won't take up much of your time; all of them can be made in less than 30 minutes. There are so many pasta shapes and sizes available which means endless combinations and possibilities. Match up your favourites with the sauces in this book, which all have low Points and fresh, luscious flavours.

Basic Recipes

Here are four recipes to help you create quick, tasty pizzas and scrumptious bowls of pasta – all lower in Points and Calories than the average shop-bought or restaurant equivalents.

Basic Tomato Sauce

This sauce is suitable for both pizzas and pasta.

Preparation time: 5 minutes + 45 minutes cooking
Freezing: recommended
Points per serving: 0
Total Points per recipe: 0
Total Calories per recipe: 135

Ⓥ

2 × 400 g (14 oz) cans of chopped tomatoes
2 garlic cloves, crushed
3 artificial sweeteners
grated zest of 1/2 lemon
2 tablespoons chopped fresh parsley
salt and freshly ground black pepper

❶ Place all the ingredients, except the parsley, in a saucepan.

❷ Bring to the boil. Reduce the heat and simmer, uncovered, for 45 minutes, until the sauce is thick and pulpy. Add the parsley and leave to cool.

❸ Purée in a blender or food processor for a smoother sauce or use as it is..

Chunky Tomato Sauce

Where would pasta be without tomato sauce? This one is extra good since it is full of chunks of vegetables.

Serves: 4
Preparation and cooking time: 35 minutes
Freezing: recommended
Points per serving: 0
Total Points per recipe: 0
Calories per serving: 55

Ⓥ

1 small onion, chopped finely
2 celery sticks, chopped finely (with leaves if possible)
1 carrot, chopped finely
3 tablespoons tomato purée
1 garlic clove, crushed
2 × 400 g (14 oz) cans of chopped tomatoes
125 ml (4 fl oz) tomato juice
150 ml (1/4 pint) vegetable stock
salt and freshly ground black pepper

❶ Put all the ingredients together in a large saucepan, bring to the boil and leave to simmer for 30 minutes, uncovered. Check the seasoning.

Basic Cheese Sauce

Cheese sauce is the delight of pasta lovers and this one has a hint of mustard for some extra flavour. Remember to add the Points for the pasta.

Serves: 4
Preparation and cooking time: 15 minutes
Freezing: recommended
Points per serving: 3
Total Points per recipe: 12
Calories per serving: 145

Ⓥ if using vegetarian cheese and margarine

1 tablespoon soft margarine
1 tablespoon plain flour
425 g (3/4 pint) skimmed milk
100 g (31/2 oz) half-fat Cheddar cheese, grated
1/2 teaspoon ready-made mustard
salt and freshly ground black pepper

❶ Melt the margarine in a large pan.
❷ Stir in the flour and cook for 2 minutes on a low heat, stirring all the time.
❸ Remove from the heat and gradually whisk in the milk.

❹ Return to the heat and bring to the boil, whisking constantly, until it thickens. Simmer for 3 minutes.
❺ Stir in the cheese, mustard and seasoning and stir until the cheese melts. Use as required.

Plain Scone Pizza Base

Use this as a base for any of the medium-size pizzas. Cook for the same length of time and at the same temperature as a pizza with a ready-made base. Use half the quantities to make a mini pizza.

Serves: 2
Preparation time: 15 minutes
Freezing: not recommended
Points per serving: with polyunsaturated margarine 9; with hard margarine 10; with butter 12
Total Points per recipe: with polyunsaturated margarine 18; with hard margarine 20; with butter 24
Calories per serving: 580

225 g (8 oz) white self-raising flour
50 g (1³/₄ oz) margarine or butter
150 ml (¹/₄ pint) skimmed milk
salt and freshly ground black pepper

Ⓥ if using vegetarian margarine

❶ Sift the flour in a large bowl with the salt and pepper. Add the margarine or butter and rub in with your fingertips, until the mixture resembles fine breadcrumbs.
❷ Stir in the milk to form a soft dough. Turn out on to a lightly floured surface and knead gently.
❸ Roll out into a 20–25 cm (8–10 inch) round circle. Line a heavy baking sheet with baking parchment or greaseproof paper and transfer the pizza base to it.

Variation: stir 2 tablespoons of any chopped fresh herb or 1 tablespoon of any dried herb into the crumb mixture, before adding the milk.

Basic Cheese Sauce (page 7)
Chunky Tomato Sauce (page 7)
Plain Scone Pizza Base

Pizzas

I n this chapter you'll find pizzas to suit every taste. We start with the mini pizzas which are very quick to cook and great for just one person. You can use almost anything as a topping. As an alternative to shop-bought mini pizzas bases, use a mini pitta bread. (A mini pitta bread is 1 Point.)

The medium-size thin and crispy pizzas serve two as a main course. Vegetarians and vegetable-lovers alike will enjoy the Vegetarian Pizza and the Margarita Pizza. The Four Seasons Pizza, the Tuna Pizza and the Asparagus and Ham Pizza are all wonderful blends of familiar and not-so-familiar flavours. Pizza Bianca is a tasty alternative to the usual garlic bread which can be served in slices with a salad or even with a pasta dish.

Deep-pan pizzas are the all-time favourite with Americans, whereas the thin and crispy pizzas are more like the real thing in Italy. But thank goodness for deep-pan pizzas; they are thick, deeply satisfying and piled high with taste. The thicker base and sides of the deep-pan pizza form a shallow case which allows it to hold more topping. I have included some medium-size deep-pan pizzas, which serve two, and some large deep-pan pizzas which serve four.

Type of base	Serves	Points per serving	Total Points
Plain scone pizza base (page 8)	2	9–12	18–24
Mini pizza base*	1	$3^1/2$	$3^1/2$
Medium pizza base*	2	$3^1/2$	7
Medium thin and crispy pizza base*	2	3	6
Medium deep-pan pizza base*	2	4	8
Large deep-pan pizza base*	4	$2^1/2$	10

Use the Plain Scone Pizza Base recipe (page 8) if you want to make your own base for any of the pizzas, except the deep pan ones; otherwise, you can substitute any of the above which are available in the supermarket.

Cook pizzas on a heavy baking sheet, lined with baking parchment or greaseproof paper, for a crisp base.

*Points calculated for supermarket own-brand pizza bases.

Seasonings for Pizzas

For added flavour, as they come out of the oven, drizzle balsamic vinegar sparingly over any of the pizzas.

Sprinkle any of the following seasonings over the cooked pizzas or add them instead of salt and freshly ground black pepper before cooking. None of these flavoured salts contain any Points.

Chilli salt: grind one dried chilli with 3 tablespoons of coarse sea salt.

Herb salt: grind one tablespoon of dried herb with 3 tablespoons of coarse sea salt. Choose from rosemary, thyme, basil, tarragon, mint or oregano.

Lemon or garlic salt: grind the finely grated zest of lemon with 2 tablespoons of coarse sea salt. Grind 3 garlic cloves with 3 tablespoons of coarse sea salt.
Hot peppers: grind one chopped dried chilli with 2 tablespoons of black peppercorns.

Light Garlic Bread

Nothing beats hot garlicky bread! This recipe lets you try it with a pizza base or pitta bread.

Serves: 1
Preparation time: 5 minutes + 10 minutes cooking
Freezing: recommended
Points per serving: 6 with pizza; 5 with pitta bread
Calories per serving: 300

Ⓥ

1 mini pizza base or medium-size pitta bread
1 tablespoon olive oil
1 garlic clove, crushed

❶ Preheat the oven to Gas Mark 5/190°C/375°F. Bake the pizza base for 10 minutes.
❷ Brush the olive oil on the base and top with the garlic. Serve warm.

Cook's note: brush the oil on to the cooked base with a pastry brush.

Variation: when using a pitta bread, just pop into the toaster and then add the oil and garlic when hot.

Italian Ham and Cheese Pizza

Figs and cottage cheese are refreshingly different toppings – pair this pizza with a tomato salad when you're in the mood for a change.

Serves: 1
Preparation time: 10 minutes + 10 minutes cooking
Freezing: not recommended
Points per serving: 5
Calories per serving: 310

1 mini pizza base
55 g (2 oz) diet plain cottage cheese, sieved
2 slices of wafer-thin ham
1 fresh fig, cut into wedges
6 watercress sprigs
salt and freshly ground black pepper

❶ Preheat the oven to Gas Mark 5/190°C/375°F.
❷ Spread the pizza base with cottage cheese.
❸ Top with the ham and fig wedges and bake for 10 minutes, until the crust is golden.
❹ Scatter over the watercress and seasoning to serve.

Variation: ripe pear can be used to replace the fig. Use ¹/₂ pear per pizza; remove the core and roughly chop the flesh.

Red Onion Pizza

Sweet red onions, garlic and basil topped with gooey mozzarella are a simple and tasty treat which you can enjoy either as a supper with a salad, or for lunch.

Serves: 1
Preparation time: 5 minutes + 20 minutes cooking
Freezing: recommended
Points per serving: 5¹/₂
Calories per serving: 285

¹/₂ large red onion, peeled and cut into wedges
1 garlic clove, chopped finely
1 tablespoon low-fat plain fromage frais
1 mini pizza base
3 fresh basil leaves or ¹/₂ teaspoon dried basil
15 g (¹/₂ oz) half-fat mozzarella cheese, grated
salt and freshly ground black pepper

❶ Preheat the oven to Gas Mark 5/190°C/375°F.
❷ Roast the onion wedges and garlic in a roasting tin for 10 minutes.
❸ Spread the fromage frais on the pizza base.
❹ Top with the roasted onion wedges and sprinkle on the basil and cheese.
❺ Bake for 10 minutes, until the cheese has melted and the crust is golden. Grind over the seasoning and serve at once.

Cook's note: to reheat a frozen pizza, thaw it first and then place it in an oven preheated to Gas Mark 5/190°C/375°F. Heat it for 5 minutes wrapped in foil and for 5 minutes without the foil.

Light Breakfast Pizza

Pizza for breakfast? Why not start the day with something to wake up your tastebuds – smoked salmon and fromage frais are a delicious alternative to toast and jam, and perfect for special occasions!

Serves: 1
Preparation time: 5 minutes + 10 minutes cooking
Freezing: not recommended
Points per serving: 6
Calories per serving: 300

1 mini pizza base
1 tablespoon chopped fresh coriander
2 tablespoons low-fat plain fromage frais
25 g (1 oz) smoked salmon, cut into strips
1 lemon wedge
freshly ground black pepper

❶ Preheat the oven to Gas Mark 5/190°C/375°F.
❷ Bake the pizza base for 10 minutes, until golden.
❸ Mix together the coriander and fromage frais.

❹ Top the warm base with the fromage frais and smoked salmon. Squeeze over the lemon juice and season with pepper.

Mini Tomato and Spinach Pizza

Pine kernels add a bit of flair to this delicious tomato and spinach topping.

Serves: 1
Preparation time: 5 minutes + 15 minutes cooking
Freezing: not recommended
Points per serving: 5
Calories per serving: 295

1 mini pizza base
2 tablespoons Basic Tomato Sauce (page 6)
55 g (2 oz) spinach
55 g (2 oz) quark (low-fat soft cheese)
6 pine kernels
salt and freshly ground black pepper

Ⓥ

❶ Preheat the oven to Gas Mark 5/190°C/375°F.
❷ Spread the pizza base with tomato sauce.
❸ Wash the spinach and heat in a saucepan, until it wilts.

❹ Top the tomato with the spinach, quark and pine kernels. Season well and bake for 15 minutes.

Margarita Pizza

The combination of tomato and basil is a favourite with Italians.

Serves: 2
Preparation time: 5 minutes + 15 minutes cooking
Freezing: not recommended
Points per serving: 5
Total Points per recipe: 10
Calories per serving: 205

1 medium-size thin and crispy pizza base
3 tablespoons Basic Tomato Sauce (page 6)
75 g (2³/₄ oz) ricotta cheese
1 tomato, sliced
1 tablespoon chopped fresh basil or 1 teaspoon dried basil

❶ Preheat the oven to Gas Mark 7/220°C/425°F.

❷ Spread the pizza base with tomato sauce. Sprinkle over the ricotta. Top with tomato slices and basil.

❸ Bake for 15 minutes, until crisp.

Basil

Margarita Pizza
Asparagus and Ham Pizza (page 18)

16

Asparagus and Ham Pizza

A spring and summer delight when asparagus is in its prime. When you buy asparagus, make sure the buds are tight and the spears have an even colour and appear firm and unwrinkled.

Serves: 2
Preparation time: 5 minutes + 15 minutes cooking
Freezing: not recommended
Points per serving: 4¹/₂
Total Points per recipe: 9
Calories per serving: 220

4 fresh asparagus spears or 4 canned spears, each cut into 3 pieces
1 medium-size thin and crispy pizza base
2 tablespoons Basic Tomato Sauce (page 6)
1 tomato, sliced
50 g (1³/₄ oz) half-fat mozzarella cheese, grated
¹/₂ teaspoon dried oregano
25 g (1 oz) wafer-thin slices of ham
salt and freshly ground black pepper

1 Preheat the oven to Gas Mark 7/220°C/425°F.

2 Boil the fresh asparagus for 3 minutes. Drain well and refresh under cold water. Drain again.

3 Spread the base with tomato sauce.

4 Top with the asparagus and tomato and then sprinkle over the cheese and oregano and top with ham.

5 Season well. Bake for 15 minutes, until crisp.

Vegetarian Pizza

This pizza is piled high with tasty vegetables but not with Calories: one of the great things about vegetables when you are trying to lose weight is that they are a no-Points food!

Serves: 2
Preparation time: 5 minutes + 25 minutes cooking
Freezing: not recommended
Points per serving: 7
Total Points per recipe: 14
Calories per serving: 310

Ⓥ

1 leek, sliced
1 courgette, sliced
1 onion, cut into thin wedges
1 tablespoon chopped fresh rosemary or
   1 teaspoon dried rosemary
3 tablespoons low-fat plain fromage frais
1 medium-size thin and crispy pizza base
   (suitable for vegetarians)
100 g (3¹/₂ oz) half-fat vegetarian mozzarella
   cheese, grated
salt and freshly ground black pepper

❶ Preheat the oven to Gas Mark 7/220°C/425°F.
❷ Mix the leek, courgette and onion in a shallow roasting tin. Roast for 15 minutes.
❸ Season well and stir in the rosemary.

❹ Spread fromage frais over the base. Top with the roasted vegetables and sprinkle with the cheese.
❺ Bake for 10 minutes, until crisp and golden. Season and serve as soon as possible.

Rosemary

Tuna Pizza

This is a nutritious and filling choice for a supper dish. Lots of texture and taste here.

Serves: 2
Preparation time: 5 minutes + 15 minutes cooking
Freezing: not recommended
Points per serving: 4¹/₂
Total Points per recipe: 9
Calories per serving: 270

1 medium-size thin and crispy pizza base
3 tablespoons Basic Tomato Sauce (page 6)
1 small onion, sliced
55 g (2 oz) mushrooms, sliced
100 g (3¹/₂ oz) can of tuna in water, drained and flaked
25 g (1 oz) sweetcorn kernels, or artichoke hearts, sliced (optional)
40 g (1¹/₂ oz) half-fat mozzarella cheese, grated
salt and freshly ground black pepper

1 Preheat the oven to Gas Mark 7/220°C/425°F.
2 Spread the pizza base with tomato sauce.
3 Top with the onion, mushrooms, tuna and sweetcorn or artichokes, if using. Sprinkle over the cheese and season.
4 Bake for 15 minutes, until crisp.

Neapolitan Pizza

This classic pizza from Naples has the rich and sensuous flavours of southern Italy.

Serves: 2
Preparation time: 10 minutes + 15 minutes cooking
Freezing: not recommended
Points per serving: 5¹/₂
Total Points per recipe: 11
Calories per serving: 275

¹/₂ × 55 g (2 oz) can of anchovies, drained
2 tablespoons milk
1 medium-size thin and crispy pizza base
3 tablespoons Basic Tomato Sauce (page 6)
¹/₂ teaspoon dried mixed Italian herbs
75 g (2³/₄ oz) half-fat mozzarella cheese, grated

1 Preheat the oven to Gas Mark 7/220°C/425°F.
2 Soak the anchovies in the milk for 10 minutes. Drain.
3 Spread the base with tomato sauce. Sprinkle over the herbs.
4 Sprinkle the cheese over the pizza base. Top with the anchovies and bake for 15 minutes.

Pizza Bianca

Here's something for garlic lovers. Simply scrumptious!

Serves: 2
Preparation time: 5 minutes + 10 minutes baking
Freezing: not recommended
Points per serving: 4¹/₂
Total Points per recipe: 9
Calories per serving: 185

Ⓥ

1 medium-size thin and crispy pizza base
1 tablespoon olive oil
3 garlic cloves, crushed

❶ Preheat the oven to Gas Mark 7/220°C/425°F.
❷ Brush ¹/₂ tablespoon of the oil over the base and bake for 10 minutes, or until crisp.
❸ Brush over the remaining oil and spread on the garlic.

Variation: add a teaspoon of one of the flavoured salts (pages 10–11).

Four Seasons Pizza

So many ingredients, so much flavour and such little effort!

Serves: 2
Preparation time: 5 minutes + 15 minutes cooking
Freezing: not recommended
Points per serving: 6¹/₂
Total Points per recipe: 13
Calories per serving: 295

1 medium-size thin and crispy pizza base
2 tablespoons Basic Tomato Sauce (page 6)
100 g (3¹/₂ oz) half-fat mozzarella cheese, grated
25 g (1 oz) mushrooms, sliced
1 tablespoon stoned black olives, sliced thinly
25 g (1 oz) spicy sausage, cut into matchsticks
¹/₂ teaspoon dried oregano
1 teaspoon capers
freshly ground black pepper

❶ Preheat the oven to Gas Mark 7/220°C/425°F.
❷ Spread the pizza base with tomato sauce.
❸ Sprinkle over the cheese. Top with mushrooms, olives, sausage, oregano and capers.

❹ Bake for 15 minutes. Season with pepper and serve hot.

Peperonata Pizza

When roasting these sweet peppers, don't worry about the charred skin – when it is peeled off, it leaves the pepper juicy with a heavenly, smoky flavour.

Serves: 3
Preparation time: 10 minutes + 25 minutes cooking
Freezing: recommended
Points per serving: 3¹/₂
Total Points per recipe: 10¹/₂
Calories per serving: 230

Ⓥ

1 red pepper, halved
1 yellow pepper, halved
1 small aubergine, sliced thinly
1 tablespoon chopped fresh thyme or 1 teaspoon dried thyme
1 medium-size deep-pan pizza base
6 tablespoons Basic Tomato Sauce (page 6)
75 g (2³/₄ oz) half-fat mozzarella cheese, grated

❶ Preheat the oven to Gas Mark 7/220°C/425°F.
❷ Place the peppers, cut-side down, on a heavy baking sheet, with the aubergine. Roast for 15 minutes.
❸ Rest the peppers by wrapping them in clingfilm or placing them in a polythene bag for 5 minutes.

Then remove the seeds and blackened skins. Cut the flesh into strips. Mix in the thyme.
❹ Spread the pizza base with tomato sauce. Top with aubergine slices and pepper strips. Sprinkle with cheese.
❺ Bake for 20 minutes until crisp.

Thyme

Peperonata Pizza

Spicy Prawn Pizza

Buy peeled and cooked prawns to save you time preparing this seafood delight with a bit of kick!

Serves: 3
Preparation time: 5 minutes + 18 minutes cooking
Freezing: not recommended
Points per serving: 4
Total Points per recipe: 12
Calories per serving: 225

1 medium-size deep-pan pizza base
6 tablespoons Basic Tomato Sauce (page 6)
100 g (3¹/₂ oz) peeled, cooked prawns
1 teaspoon Tabasco sauce or to taste
75 g (2³/₄ oz) half-fat mozzarella cheese, grated
¹/₂ teaspoon dried oregano

1 Preheat the oven to Gas Mark 7/220°C/425°F.
2 Spread the pizza base with tomato sauce.
3 Mix together the prawns with Tabasco sauce to taste.

4 Scatter the prawns over the base. Sprinkle over the mozzarella and oregano.
5 Bake for 15–18 minutes, until crisp.

Oregano

Ham and Mushroom Pizza

Marinating the mushrooms in garlic and vinegar makes the great taste of ham and mushroom pizza even better.

Serves: 3

Preparation time: 5 minutes + 15 minutes
   marinating + 18 minutes cooking

Freezing: not recommended

Points per serving: 3

Total Points per recipe: 9

Calories per serving: 155

100 g (3¹/₂ oz) field mushrooms, sliced

1 tablespoon red wine vinegar

1 garlic clove, crushed

1 medium-size deep-pan pizza base

3 tablespoons Basic Tomato Sauce (page 6)

25 g (1 oz) wafer-thin ham

25 g (1 oz) stoned black olives, sliced

1 Preheat the oven to Gas Mark 7/220°C/425°F.

2 Mix the mushrooms with the vinegar and garlic and marinate for 15 minutes.

3 Spread the pizza base with tomato sauce. Drain the mushrooms and arrange them on top. Add the ham and olives and bake for 15–18 minutes, until crisp

Hot and Spicy Pizza

Spice, spice and more spice in this pizza – definitely not for the fainthearted! If you're not keen on spicy food, reduce the quantity of chilli or leave it out altogether.

Serves: 4
Preparation time: 15 minutes + 25 minutes
  cooking
Freezing: not recommended
Points per serving: 5¹/₂
Total Points per recipe: 22
Calories per serving: 355

225 g (8 oz) extra-lean minced beef
2 tablespoons barbecue sauce
4 tablespoons tomato juice
6 tablespoons Basic Tomato Sauce (page 6)
1 large deep-pan pizza base
1 fresh red chilli, de-seeded and chopped finely
1 fresh green chilli, de-seeded and chopped finely
25 g (1 oz) spicy sausage, cut into matchsticks
75 g (2³/₄ oz) half-fat mozzarella cheese, grated

❶ Preheat the oven to Gas Mark 7/220°C/425°F.
❷ Heat a frying-pan and brown the mince for 2–3 minutes. Add the barbecue sauce and tomato juice and simmer for 10 minutes.
❸ Spoon the tomato sauce on to the pizza base. Add the mince mixture.

❹ Top with the chillies and spicy sausage and sprinkle over the cheese.
❺ Bake for 20–25 minutes, until crisp. Serve immediately.

Chillies

Marinara Pizza

The silvery anchovy has a deliciously strong and piquant flavour – here it is soaked in milk to remove some of the saltiness.

Serves: 4
Preparation time: 10 minutes + 25 minutes cooking
Freezing: not recommended
Points per serving: 3^1/$_2$
Total Points per recipe: 14
Calories per serving: 270

50 g (1³/₄ oz) can of anchovies, drained
2 tablespoons milk
1 large deep-pan pizza base
5 tablespoons Basic Tomato Sauce (page 6)
2 garlic cloves, crushed
**100 g (3¹/₂ oz) can of tuna in brine, drained
    and flaked**
2 tomatoes, sliced
1 teaspoon dried oregano
50 g (1³/₄ oz) stoned black olives, sliced

❶ Preheat the oven to Gas Mark 7/220°C/425°F.
❷ Soak the anchovies in the milk for 10 minutes.
❸ Meanwhile, spread the pizza base with tomato sauce. Scatter over the garlic and tuna. Top with

tomato slices, oregano and olives. Lastly, arrange the anchovies decoratively.
❹ Bake for 20–25 minutes, until crisp.

Mixed Vegetable Pizza

Eat healthily, and enjoy the textures and flavours of fresh vegetables along with sweetcorn which is high in carbohydrate and contains protein and vitamins A and C.

Serves: 4
Preparation time: 5 minutes + 20 minutes cooking
Freezing: not recommended
Points per serving: 3
Total Points per recipe: 12
Calories per serving: 245

Ⓥ if using vegetarian mozzarella

1 large deep-pan pizza base
6 tablespoons Basic Tomato Sauce (page 6)
2 garlic cloves, crushed
1 onion, sliced finely
50 g (1³/₄ oz) button mushrooms, sliced
1 small red pepper, de-seeded and sliced finely
1 small green pepper, de-seeded and sliced finely
1 tablespoon sweetcorn kernels
50 g (1¹/₂ oz) half-fat mozzarella cheese, grated

❶ Preheat the oven to Gas Mark 7/220°C/425°F.
❷ Spread the pizza base with tomato sauce.

❸ Top with garlic, onion, mushrooms, peppers and sweetcorn. Top with mozzarella and bake for 20 minutes, until crisp.

Marinara Pizza
Mixed Vegetable Pizza

Pasta

Pasta has so much going for it. It is quick, easy to prepare and economical. It is also nourishing, easily digested, and releases energy over a long period of time. Best of all though, it has a low fat content, is very satisfying and tastes great.

When you are losing weight, watch the Points of the pasta sauce – it's the real culprit. With this in mind, I have created some tasty low-Point sauces for you to enjoy with any size or shape of pasta. I have included suggestions of pasta to accompany many of the sauces but please feel free to experiment and try your own variations and do remember to add the Points for the pasta in recipes which give Points for sauces only.

To make the pasta, allow 50 g (1³/₄ oz) of dried pasta per person and 75 g (2³/₄ oz) of fresh pasta per person. All packets of dried pasta carry clear cooking instructions but here are some standard instructions for your reference. Bring a large saucepan of water to a good rolling boil, add about 1 tablespoon of salt and toss in the pasta. (Pasta needs to be cooked in lots of boiling water so it can tumble freely and not stick together.) Bring the water and pasta back to the boil and cook for the recommended time. Drain immediately and tip straight back into the pan, so it is still slightly wet. Toss in the prepared sauce and mix well. Serve immediately.

Leek and Bacon Pasta Sauce

Leeks first appear in the autumn and early winter and are deservedly a much-loved vegetable. Their delicate flavour makes them the perfect accompaniment to savoury bacon in this pasta sauce. Serve with your favourite pasta shapes, remembering to add the Points.

Serves: 4
Preparation and cooking time: 25 minutes
Freezing: not recommended
Points per serving: 5¹/₂
Total Points per recipe: 22
Calories per serving: 200

1 quantity of Basic Cheese Sauce (page 7)
4 rashers of lean back bacon, cut into pieces
2 leeks, sliced
125 g (4 oz) broccoli, cut into small florets
salt and freshly ground black pepper

1 Make the cheese sauce.
2 Heat a large pan, add the bacon and leeks and fry for about 2 minutes.

3 Stir in the broccoli and cook for 2 minutes.
4 Add the cheese sauce, season to taste and gently simmer for 3 minutes.

Mushroom Pasta Sauce

This medley of mushrooms creates an intense savoury sauce. Mushrooms have a lot to offer; not only do they taste wonderful, they have low salt, no cholesterol and no fat! They also have lots of important vitamins and minerals. Serve with any pasta shape, remembering to add the Points.

Serves: 4

Preparation and cooking time: 25 minutes

Freezing: not recommended

Points per serving: 3

Total Points per recipe: 12

Calories per serving: 155

1 quantity of Basic Cheese Sauce (page 7)

50 g (1³/₄ oz) button mushrooms, chopped finely

75 g (2³/₄ oz) chestnut mushrooms, sliced or cut into wedges

100 g (3¹/₂ oz) field mushrooms, sliced

2 tablespoons chopped fresh parsley

Ⓥ if using vegetarian Basic Cheese Sauce

❶ Make the cheese sauce, adding all the mushrooms to the melted margarine. Cook them for 2 minutes before adding the flour.

❷ Add the parsley and cheese.

Pasta Bows with Chicken and Sage Sauce

Sage flourishes in the Mediterranean where the heat of the sun concentrates its aromatic oils and makes it a lovely complement to other Mediterranean flavours. Here it is delicious with chicken and red wine.

Serves: 4
Preparation and cooking time: 20 minutes
Freezing: not recommended
Points per serving: 4$^1/_2$
Total Points per recipe: 18
Calories per serving: 310

225 g (8 oz) dried pasta bows
For the sauce:
2 medium-size boneless, skinless chicken
    breasts, cooked and cut into bite-size pieces
1 small onion, chopped finely
1 tablespoon chopped fresh sage
125 ml (4 fl oz) red wine
3 tablespoons low-fat plain fromage frais
salt and freshly ground black pepper

❶ Place the chicken, onion and sage in a frying-pan, with the red wine. Simmer, uncovered, for 10 minutes.

❷ Meanwhile, cook the pasta according to the packet instructions. Drain.

❸ Mix the chicken mixture, pasta and fromage frais together. Season and serve immediately.

Farfalle

Red Pepper Pesto and Cannelloni

Cannelloni is Italian comfort food – it can be stuffed with such tasty and filling ingredients.
In this recipe it oozes with cheese, red peppers and aubergines.

Serves: 4

Preparation time: 25 minutes + 20 minutes baking

Freezing: not recommended

Points per serving: 2

Total Points per recipe: 8

Calories per serving: 345

Ⓥ if using vegetarian ricotta

2 red peppers, halved

1 aubergine, chopped roughly

2 unpeeled garlic cloves

2 tablespoons chopped fresh basil or 2 teaspoons dried basil

50 g (1³/₄ oz) fresh white breadcrumbs

75 g (2³/₄ oz) ricotta cheese, crumbled

freshly grated nutmeg

For the cannelloni:

12 cannelloni tubes

1 quantity of Chunky Tomato Sauce (page 7)

❶ Preheat the oven to Gas Mark 7/220°C/425°F.

❷ Place the peppers, cut-side down, with the aubergine and garlic on a heavy baking tray and roast in the oven for 10 minutes, until the pepper skins are well blackened.

❸ Cover the peppers and garlic with clingfilm or put in a polythene bag and leave to cool. Peel the peppers and remove the seeds. Peel the roasted garlic.

❹ Place the pepper flesh, garlic and basil in a food processor and blend until smooth. Stir in the breadcrumbs, aubergine and ricotta and season with nutmeg.

❺ Stuff this mixture into cannelloni tubes, place in a baking dish and top with tomato sauce. Bake for 20 minutes, until the pasta is soft.

Variation: cook 225 g (8 oz) dried pasta shapes, according to the packet instructions. Add to the aubergine mixture and tomato sauce in a large saucepan and heat through. Points will be 3¹/₂ per serving.

Red Pepper Pesto and Cannelloni
Pasta Bows with Chicken and Sage Sauce (page 35)

Chinese Pasta with Cucumber Relish

Some say it wasn't the Italians who invented pasta, but the Chinese. Capelli is fine, long spaghetti which is probably not unlike the original Chinese pasta which evolved into the well-known noodle. Capelli is often sold in small, nest-like bunches and is mouth-watering with these oriental flavours.

Serves: 4

Preparation and cooking time: 25 minutes

Freezing: not recommended

Points per serving: 3

Total Points per recipe: 12

Calories per serving: 275

225 g (8 oz) capelletti pasta

3 spring onions, chopped finely

2.5 cm (1-inch) piece of fresh root ginger, peeled and grated

1 garlic clove, crushed

2 tablespoons light soy sauce

2 tablespoons dry sherry

175 g (6 oz) peeled, cooked prawns

For the relish:

$^1/_2$ cucumber, cut into small cubes

1 red pepper, de-seeded and chopped finely

finely grated zest and juice of 1 lime

salt and freshly ground black pepper

❶ Cook the pasta in a large pan of salted, boiling water.

❷ Place the onions, ginger, garlic, soy sauce and sherry in a wok or large frying-pan and simmer for 3 minutes.

❸ Meanwhile, make the relish and mix the cucumber, pepper, lime zest and juice together and season well.

❹ Add the prawns to the onion mixture and heat for 2 minutes.

❺ Drain the pasta and mix with the prawn mixture.

❻ Serve the pasta in bowls, with a tablespoon of cucumber relish on top.

Variation: add a fresh red chilli, de-seeded and finely chopped, instead of the pepper, for a hotter relish.

Pasta Shells with Salmon and Salsa

Intensely aromatic peppercorns, salmon steak and coriander fill these pasta shells with loads of flavour.

Serves: 4
Preparation and cooking time: 20 minutes
Freezing: not recommended
Points per serving: 3½
Total Points per recipe: 14
Calories per serving: 310

225 g (8 oz) dried pasta shells
For the sauce:
225 g (8 oz) salmon steak
1 lemon
1 bay leaf
3 peppercorns
4 tomatoes, chopped roughly
½ red onion, chopped finely
finely grated zest and juice of 1 lime
2 tablespoons chopped fresh coriander
salt and freshly ground black pepper

❶ Place the salmon steak in a small pan with the juice of the lemon. Add the bay leaf, peppercorns and 3 tablespoons of water. Cook, covered, for 10 minutes. Leave in the hot water once cooked.

❷ Meanwhile, cook the pasta shells in salted boiling water, according to the packet instructions.

❸ Drain the salmon, remove the bones and skin and break up the flesh into large flakes.

❹ Heat the salmon flakes, tomatoes, red onion, lime zest and juice together for 5 minutes. Stir in the coriander and season well.

❺ Drain the pasta, mix it with the sauce and serve.

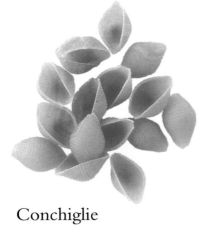

Conchiglie

Pasta Shells with Salmon and Salsa
Crab and Vegetable Pasta (page 42)

Crab and Vegetable Pasta

Very similar to fettuccine, tagliatelle are flat, ribbon noodles with a lovely thickness. If you want to spice up the mild flavour of crabmeat, try the sauce variation below.

Serves: 4

Preparation and cooking time: 20 minutes

Freezing: not recommended

Points per serving: 3½

Total Points per recipe: 14

Calories per serving: 265

225 g (8 oz) tagliatelle

2 courgettes, cut into thin ribbons

2 carrots, peeled and cut into thin ribbons

100 g (3½ oz) can of crabmeat, drained and flaked

4 tablespoons low-fat plain fromage frais

2 tablespoons tomato ketchup

salt and freshly ground black pepper

❶ Cook the tagliatelle for 12 minutes in salted, boiling water. Drain.

❷ Meanwhile, blanch the vegetables for 2 minutes in salted, boiling water; drain well. Mix with the crabmeat, fromage frais and tomato ketchup, season well and gently heat for 3 minutes.

❸ Mix with the pasta and serve.

Variation: add 1 extra tablespoon of fromage frais and a fresh red chilli, de-seeded, instead of the tomato ketchup, for a hotter sauce. Points will remain the same.

Pasta Quills with Tuna and Tomato Sauce

Always have some canned tuna on hand – it's so versatile and inexpensive. Tuna belongs to the same fish family as mackerel and is full of goodness. And pasta loves it, hot or cold.

Serves: 4
Preparation and cooking time: 20 minutes
Freezing: not recommended
Points per serving: 2¹/₂
Total Points per recipe: 10
Calories per serving: 255

225 g (8 oz) dried pasta quills
For the sauce:
1 small onion, chopped roughly
4 fresh tomatoes, chopped roughly
150 ml (¹/₄ pint) tomato juice
175 g (6 oz) fresh spinach, washed, or frozen spinach, thawed
100 g (3¹/₂ oz) can of tuna in brine, drained
salt and freshly ground black pepper

❶ Place the onion, tomatoes and tomato juice in a saucepan and simmer, uncovered, for 10 minutes stirring from time to time.

❷ Add the spinach and tuna and cook for a further 5 minutes. Season well.

❸ Meanwhile, cook the pasta in salted, boiling water, according to the packet instructions.

❹ Drain the pasta, mix with the tuna sauce and serve.

Penne

43

Tagliatelle with Garlic and Mushroom Sauce

Deliciously creamy and low in Points!

Serves: 4
Preparation and cooking time: 20 minutes
Freezing: not recommended
Points per serving: 2¹/₂
Total Points per recipe: 10
Calories per serving: 225

225 g (8 oz) green tagliatelle
75 g (2³/₄ oz) open-cup mushrooms, sliced
100 ml (3¹/₂ fl oz) vegetable stock
75 g (2³/₄ oz) low-fat garlic soft cheese
2 tablespoons chopped fresh parsley
salt and freshly ground black pepper

V if using vegetarian cream cheese

1 Cook the pasta in salted, boiling water for 2 minutes. Drain well.

2 Cook the mushrooms in the stock for 3 minutes.

3 Stir in the garlic cheese and parsley. Add the pasta and heat gently for 2 minutes. Season and serve.

Pasta Twists with Light Pesto Sauce

In Italy pesto is known as 'food for the Gods'.

Serves: 4
Preparation and cooking time: 20 minutes
Freezing: not recommended
Points per serving: 3¹/₂
Total Points per recipe: 14
Calories per serving: 255

225 g (8 oz) dried pasta twists
For the sauce:
20 fresh basil leaves or 1 teaspoon dried basil
1 red onion, peeled and chopped roughly
2 tablespoons balsamic vinegar
150 ml (¹/₄ pint) half cream
salt and freshly ground black pepper

V

1 Cook the pasta in salted, boiling water for 12 minutes. Drain.

2 In a food processor, process the basil, onion and vinegar together until smooth.

3 Mix the pesto, pasta and cream together and heat gently for 3 minutes. Season and serve.

Tagliatelle with Garlic and Mushroom Sauce

Pasta Bows with Mustardy Chicken Sauce

Nothing beats a tasty cream sauce with pasta, and mustard and chicken, together with the luxuriously soft texture of leeks, make this dish very moreish indeed!

Serves: 4
Preparation and cooking time: 20 minutes
Freezing: not recommended
Points per serving: 4
Total Points per recipe: 16
Calories per serving: 285

225 g (8 oz) dried pasta bows
750 ml (1¹/₂ pints) chicken stock
2 medium-size, skinless, boneless chicken
   breasts, cooked and cut into bite-size pieces
1 garlic clove, crushed
2 leeks, chopped finely
2 teaspoons whole-grain mustard
2 tablespoons half cream
freshly ground black pepper

1 Cook the pasta in the chicken stock. Drain, reserving the stock.

2 Meanwhile, place the chicken, garlic, leeks and mustard in a saucepan, add 200 ml (7 fl oz) of chicken stock from the cooking of the pasta and gently simmer for 5 minutes, uncovered.

3 Stir the cream into the sauce and heat for 2 minutes, uncovered. Season with black pepper and serve with the pasta.

Rotini

Pasta Bows with Mustardy Chicken Sauce

Index